Simplifying Craft Shows

-A Guide to Organizing Your Handmade Business

By
Sandra M. Belz

Table of Contents

A Brief Intro.. Page 2

Why You Need A Checklist.................. Page 3

Craft Show Checklist............................ Page 4

Keeping Track of Sales......................... Page 11

Craft Show Sales Tracker..................... Page 13

Keeping Tax Records........................... Page 16

Tax & Records Folder Organization..... Page 19

Monthly Expense Tracker.................... Page 21

Mileage Tracker.................................... Page 24

Keeping Inventory Records.................. Page 25

Final Thoughts..................................... Page 27

A Brief Intro

  I recently revised and republished my book, *A Guide to Craft Show Success,* (which I self-published through Amazon), and a few days later I had the idea to create a sort of companion guide for it that would help artisans and crafters organize their businesses using the tools that have helped me greatly over the last several years. In this guide, I offer some tips and worksheets that will help you to plan and pack for a craft show, keep track of your expenses and tax records, as well as things we sometimes don't think about, like tracking mileage and inventory.
  Much of what I have compiled here has been through my own trial and error along the way, as well as taking advice from others, which I worked into my own right-brained way of keeping records. Of course the wonderful thing about a handmade business is that it will always be uniquely your own; so by no means feel like the charts and lists that I've compiled are the end all be all. Depending on your business and what you sell, you may want to add items or drop some, change the format of a list or chart, or create something new with the ideas I've offered here. My hope is that you will find this useful in beginning your handmade business journey, or in organizing your current business for optimal success!

Why You Need A Checklist

When you're heading off to sell your amazing work at a craft show, festival or farmer's market, there are so many things you need to remember. Not only all of the lovelies you've created and packed up for the road, but several other items that will ensure the event runs smoothly for you.

First you'll want to know certain details about the event you'll be attending. Things like, will I have an indoor or outdoor space? (Some venues include both, so be sure to find out.) Do you need electricity for any reason and need to request a space equipped with an outlet? Does the event coordinator require tents if the show is outdoors? Will tables and chairs be included or do you need to bring your own? Will your set up require you to enlist the help of a partner or friend that day? Once you have all of the fundamentals covered, you want to be sure you don't leave any items behind when you head out for the show.

This checklist is a great start to ensure you have all of your bits and pieces in order for the day of an event. Depending on what you specialize in and what products you'll be taking with you to sell, you may need to add things or ignore a few things on the list provided. I'll leave spaces for you to do so.

Even after the many, many shows, markets and events that I've done, I still keep a system of organization and a list just to be sure I don't forget anything. Life is busy and often hectic, so don't feel the need to try to keep it all straight in your head. Write it down, check it off and give your brain a moment to breathe and relax.

Craft Show Checklist

- <u>Products</u> This is where you will list anything you plan to sell. All of your handmade items or resale items (if they are permitted). If you sell a variety of smaller items, it's a good idea to list them separately. For example if you sell jewelry, list: earrings, necklaces, rings, etc. If you offer skin care, list: face wash, moisturizer, toner and so on. In the rush of packing it's easy to overlook an essential!

_____

_____

_____

_____

_____

_____

_____

_____

_____

- <u>Tables</u> Consider how many tables and what size you'll need to best display your work. When first starting out, 1 fold out table may be enough and you can always add more later. Also consider the size of the event space. Coordinators usually inform vendors in advance what size of space they will have to work in, and sometimes what table size is permitted.

- <u>Chairs</u> If you're going solo, taking 1 fold out chair is plenty for you to take an occasional rest. Stools are also a nice option if you have space to pack them in your vehicle.

- <u>A Tent</u> Usually tents are optional, but occasionally required. If you are packing a tent, make sure you have all of the supplies and pieces you need to secure it. Also consider whether or not you can easily assemble it yourself, or if someone needs to go with you to help.

- <u>Display Items</u> This is where you'll jot down anything that you need or want on your table that's not for sale. These are the items that create a storefront vibe for your booth. I have started the list with some general items, but left space for you to add anything relevant to your business.

- <u>Tablecloth(s)</u>

- <u>Decorations</u>

- <u>Business card holder</u>

- <u>Signage</u> (price tags, small informational signs etc)

- <u>Shelves</u>

- <u>Tape</u> (to tape down signage if needed)

- <u>Scissors</u> (to remove tags if a customer wishes)

- <u>Display Stands</u>

- <u>Other Items</u> These are all items that don't necessarily have a special category but are also important. In the notes area, write down anything that randomly pops into your head. Handmade businesses are all wonderfully unique, so if you think it's beneficial for your display or to help your business, take it along. Write it down here so you don't forget.

_____

_____

_____

_____

_____

_____

- <u>Packaging</u> (bags, tissue paper, ribbon etc- what you need to wrap your items)

- <u>Business Cards</u>

- <u>Change/ Money bag/ Credit Card Reader/ Receipt Book(s)</u>

- <u>Snacks/ Water</u>

- <u>Notepad/ Pens</u>

- <u>Samples</u> If you sell food items, list samples you'd like to offer- or if you make skin care or other items that might lend well to a customer trying a bit.

- <u>Promotional Materials</u> For example, if you plan to do a drawing for a free gift, or are collecting emails for follow ups, you want to be sure to have the slips of paper for the drawing, raffle tickets, a clipboard for customer info etc.

- <u>A Full Tank of Gas</u> It may seem silly, but you don't want to show up late because you had to stop for gas, or worse, get stranded.

- <u>Social Media Promotion</u> Remember to share on your social media platform of choice where the show will be and what time it will be happening. Also take a few photos while there and share them either during or after the event, if you have time.

- <u>An Attitude to Rock It!</u> This isn't a tangible item to pack, but having confidence in yourself and the awesome work you do, can be the biggest part of your selling success!

- <u>Additional Items and Notes:</u>

_____

_____

_____

_____

_____

_____

_____

_____

_____

<u>Event Address:</u>   <u>Event Coordinator/Contact Person</u>

_____   _____

_____   <u>Phone Number</u>

Time and Date of the Event:

Other Notes:

Keeping Track of Sales

Whether you have already made the decision that selling your handmade work is going to be a full time income for you, or simply a hobby, I suggest keeping good records of your sales. If your dream is to quit the day job you hate by selling awesome artwork or unique jewelry, then definitely do not skip this part. Even if you feel like you're not making very much at the start, keeping a detailed record of your sales and receipts can help prevent a tax audit down the road when your business does take off. Even if you are a decided hobbyist, keeping track of your sales and expenses might be an eye opener to the potential your crafts have for legitimate income.

First and foremost I have to add the disclaimer that I am not a tax professional, an accountant or even that great at math. I do know how to keep track of money though, and that's really all you need at this point as well.

When you're at a show, selling away, it's really easy to be excited and to forget to record sales as money exchanges hands. I suggest getting into a habit of jotting down each item sold as well as the sales amount, either before you pack the customer's item or immediately after, whichever feels most comfortable for you to keep things flowing. This not only gives you a clear sum of how much money you've made at the end of the day, but also what items sold the most, letting you know what you'll need to restock before the next event. In the next section, I'll cover tracking taxes, so don't stress about that just yet.

I use small restaurant style carbon copy receipt books. They're inexpensive and you can easily find them at any office supply store, or online. This way I can easily flip my personal tracking page over and offer a handwritten credit card receipt if someone asks for one. I have known other vendors to use a spiral notebook to do the same, or they might simply put the date at the top and then keep track of each sale amount without additional notes.

Just a few thoughts on this- if you sell a variety of items in a category, like jewelry, soaps or candles, writing down the type of jewelry (as in the chart example) or the fragrance or style of candle or soap could be most beneficial in figuring out what you'll need to restock first. If you sell food or larger items like wreaths or woodwork, it's easier to see what sold by the end of the day just by memory, and detailed descriptions might not be as necessary. In the end, this all comes down to the type of business you own and what the easiest solution will be for you. As long as your sales record is easy to read and refer back to when you need it, you can't go wrong.

Craft Show Sales Tracker

Date of Show:_____

Name of Show/Location:

_____

_____

___

Item Sold	Price
ie: necklace	$25
earrings	$12
bookmark	$14
necklace + earrings	$37

Item Sold   Price

_____

_____

_____

_____

Total Items Sold: _____   Total Retail Amount Sold:$_____

Keeping Tax Records

Let's face it, no one likes taxes. Well, maybe the government likes taxes, but for the most part the rest of us tend to get intimidated and nervous about the whole subject, especially small business owners. Are you reporting everything you should be? Are you deducting the right things? Do you really have to report your crafty income anyway? Hopefully I can help clear up a little bit of the confusion for you here. Again, I am not a licensed tax professional or accountant or have any extra special knowledge about how the system works, but I do have some advice that has proven to work well for me year after year.

Before we get knee deep into it, I suggest that you find out specific regulations for your state. This is easier than you might think. Go to your state's official Department of Revenue (DOR) website and register for an Employee Identification Number (EIN). Doing this will register your business as a legitimate business with your state. Here, you'll also have access to information on any questions you might have. You'll find out exactly how much tax you'll need to collect and then return to the state on each sale. When I say "return" for each sale, I mean the tax you collect for the state is not actually your money.

For example, think about it this way: Here in North Carolina the sales tax for any items that I sell totals to 6.75% (4.75% for the state and 2% for the county). I add 6.75% to the retail I ask for each item. So when I collect $0.68 on a $10.00 sale, I haven't earned $10.68. Rather I am collecting that $0.68 for the state and giving it to them when I pay my quarterly taxes. Each state and county has varying rates, so again, be sure to check into your specific area's rates.

At the end of every quarter you'll sign into the website, log in as your business and pay whatever sales tax is due. The sales quarters breakdown like this:
- January, February, March
- April, May, June
- July, August, September
- October, November, December

Another benefit of registering your business and having an EIN is that now you'll also be able to do business with wholesalers. Purchasing your materials at wholesale costs rather than paying the markup at craft stores makes a big difference to your bottom line.

Let's say that you're just testing the waters with something you've made and you're setting up at the local church bazarre to see if the beautiful crochet baby hats you love to make would actually sell. Do you really need all of these steps? If it's a one time thing to clear out your craft room, probably not. But if you sell out and suddenly realize this could be lucrative income, you can still go back and register your business, adding in the sales from any shows or online sales you may have already made.

Something else to consider is that each state varies in how much money you actually earn before it needs to be reported as income. The last time I checked in, the minimum in North Carolina is $600. In other words, once you sell $600 of handmade items within a calendar year, it is considered income and must be reported. Again, check in with the most recent rules and specifically to your state.

When in doubt about any of this, or if you have any other questions, please speak with your personal tax professional. This should be someone who does this for a living. Filing taxes for a small business is not as simple as filing a W-2 form, which many people can do on their own. The world of taxes seems to change as often as the facebook algorithm, so working with a professional who stays up to date on all of the changes every year is only to your benefit.

On another note, Federal tax is a whole other animal, and this is definitely something you want to ask your tax professional about. A general good rule of thumb is to subtract 15%- 25% of your total profit in expectation of paying those federal deductions that come out on W-2 forms. However, when you file as a small business owner there are many, many considerations and deductions involved as well. So my advice is to save a little just in case you fall into the bracket of paying at the end of the year.

So now that we've covered a few basics, the question most handmade business owners have is- what do I actually need to keep track of? I was fortunate enough to work with a woman who was not only a professional tax preparer, but also had her own business. I attended a workshop with her on how to organize tax paperwork many years ago, and it's a system that I still use. I'm not kidding when I say that my tax man is always relieved at how easy my form is to complete because of this organized system!

You'll want to purchase some file folders- enough to cover each of these categories. Keeping good records as you go will save you from so much stress at tax time!

At the top of each folder, write down one category. Then you can organize documents, receipts and notes in each folder according to the list below each category. If it makes life easier for you, don't hesitate to write the detailed lists inside of each folder to help you remember where papers need to go.

Keep in mind that as your handmade business grows, and depending on how you might branch out in the creative world, more categories might be added. For example if you are starting a YouTube channel and it takes off, you might end up receiving dividends from your work there. Or if you write a book, (wink, wink) be sure to keep records of all royalties you receive. Add categories as you need them. I feel that more is better when it comes to organizing paperwork!

Tax and Records Folder Organization

Monthly Totals and Receipts
- Craft show trackers from each show
- Written receipts of sales
- Printouts/ receipts from any online website sales (ie: Etsy)
- Receipts/ trackers from any other sales (friends, through facebook, instagram, etc.
- Income from any workshops you might teach*
- Records of any other income associated with your handmade or creative business*

Prize Earnings
- Records of any earnings from contests
- Records of any free materials won in a contest or giveaway

Supplies and Materials
- Receipts for all materials you purchase to create items with
  - Keep in mind smaller items as well, such as needles, thread, buttons, pens, pencils, markers, paper, etc; anything that you legitimately use as part of your process in making the items that you sell.
- Tools required for creating items
- Machinery that may be required for making the items you sell

Advertising

This folder is for receipts and records for anything that promotes your business, such as:

- Business cards
- Labels or stickers (for bags or boxes)
- Copies or fliers
- Banners and signage
- Facebook, Instagram or other online ads
- Displays: Tables, shelves, decorative items for shows, etc.
- Door prizes or giveaways (record the retail price of an item)

Office Supplies and Postage

- Stationary or printer paper used for the business
- Printer Ink (if used for your business)
- Paper clips, staples, pens and other general office supplies
- Postage stamps
- Shipping costs: mailers, tissue papers, tape, ribbon, etc (anything used to mail orders)
- Shipping receipts- (receipts and reports for mailed items)
- Receipt pads
- Notebooks- for record keeping
- File folders

Fees

- Vendor or booth payments
- Commissions (the percentage or rent you pay to store owners who sell your work in their shops)
- Credit card fees (how much the company charges you for use)
- Fees for using Paypal, Venmo, Cashapp or any other parties you might use to collect money
- Etsy seller fees or what you pay monthly/ yearly for a personal website or blog

Travel Expenses and Mileage

- A record of mileage to and from shows, events, workshops, etc. (I keep a small notebook in my car to write this down throughout the year)
- Parking receipts (ie: if you pay parking in a garage at an event or class you're teaching)
- If selling at an out of town event, keep receipts and records for:
  - Hotel costs
  - Meals (can be deducted up to 50%)
  - Gas receipts (prices sometimes vary if going out of state)

*If you teach workshops or classes where you share your creative skills, you can usually lump these earnings in with your handmade business. You are considered a private contractor, and this is a good place to keep these records. Keep in mind however, that taxes from this sort of work are different from collecting sales tax on items you sell. Definitely speak with your accountant or tax professional for details on this type of income and how you will report it at the end of a quarter or year. Again, these things may also vary from state to state

Monthly Expense Tracker

As an artist I find that the more organized I keep all of my records and files, the easier I breathe. Paperwork stresses me out! So knowing that all of my i's are dotted and my t's are crossed provides me with a sense of calm that allows me to work my business with more freedom. I personally like to have easy to reference files so that if I need to check something, I know that I won't have to spend too much time and energy looking for it. I would much rather spend that time and energy being creative!

For this reason, in addition to the file folders where I put every receipt and report, I also keep an online spreadsheet record of each month's numbers. Not only does this guarantee that there is an online copy of my records, in case (all things forbid) my papers are somehow ruined or lost, but it's also an easy way for me to track progress in my business from month to month. I can easily see whether or not my sales are increasing or decreasing each month, which can be a reason to celebrate or a little boost of motivation to change something. Looking back through these from year to year also offers some insight into patterns. For example if you look back and notice that January tends to be a much slower month for sales and that things don't pick up again until October you can ask yourself, why? Of course, this is something that will vary depending on what products you offer as well; whether they are more seasonal or whether you only sell at craft shows a few months of the year. Considering all of these factors, maybe it could offer insight into how to produce sales in typically slower months.

Below I am sharing the system that I have used for years. I'll be noting the basics and, as I mentioned in the previous section, as your business grows and you possibly add other streams of income, you'll want to add those to your chart as well. I'll list the categories I use at the top of the page and a few examples. I suggest filling them into columns on a spreadsheet to keep things neat and easier to look at. I use Google Docs because it's what I am most familiar with, but any program you choose should work as well.

I suggest listing each month of the year on the left side of your spreadsheet grouped into the business quarters in which they fall. This makes it simple to add up at the end of each quarter to pay taxes. List each category across the top, filling in your state's tax requirements. I am using North Carolina's information for example purposes.

Suggested categories for the top of your spreadsheet:

- Total Retail Sales: These are sales of all items sold, no matter what the platform. All of your retail sales before tax from craft shows, a website, through social media, stores, etc. This is how I choose to keep track, but of course feel free to break it down further if you prefer.

- 4.75% tax : The first portion of tax I report for NC, this is the state sales tax. Check for your state's rates.
- 2 % tax: This is the county tax that I report for NC. I keep these recorded separately because it makes it easier to input into the system each quarter.

- Etsy Fees: This is a total monthly sum of listing fees and the percentage Etsy takes from each sale of your items.

- Other Website Fees: If you have a personal website through a platform like Shopify for example, this is where you would input the monthly cost of the site as well as any fees they might deduct from your sales, etc.

- Postage/Shipping: Add up shipping receipts and input the monthly total here. This is not packaging cost- just the actual cost to ship items. *

- Materials: Any supplies and tools that you purchase to make your handmade items goes here.* This isn't a detailed breakdown, it just offers perspective on how much you spend on supplies vs. how much is selling.

- Vendor Fees: If you've participated in craft shows or if you rent a space in a storefront setting, enter your total costs in this section.

- Mileage : Add up your total mileage for the month and keep note of it in this column for your records. I find it's easier to do this month by month, rather than add all of these totals at one time at the end of the year. These are numbers that can pile up, so I personally find it less overwhelming to record them in smaller chunks.

- Parking Fees: If you are at events where you have to pay for parking on a regular basis, keep track of it month to month. If this is a once in a blue moon occurrence, simply add the receipts to your travel tax folder. For example I often teach camps and workshops in downtown Greensboro, where I need to park in a parking deck for the day. As with mileage, I just find it easier to tally these each month.

- <u>Income from Workshops etc.:</u> If you teach classes, workshops or do other events where you are paid for your creative brain, but aren't selling actual items, you can keep track of that income in this column throughout the year. This is a good way to total up your income from these events and keep an eye on how much you should estimate for taxes.

Then on the left of your spreadsheet:
- January
  February   -Quarter 1
  March

- April
  May   -Quarter 2
  June

- July
  August   -Quarter 3
  September

- October
  November   -Quarter 4
  December

Here is an example of what a portion of your chart might look like:

	Total Retail Sales	4.75% tax	2% tax	Etsy fees	Booth/Fees
January	$782	$37.15	$15.64	N/A	$200.00
February	$830	$39.43	$16.60	$25.00	$75.00
March	$900	$42.75	$18.00	$35.00	$180.00
Quarterly Totals:	$2,512	$119.33	$32.42	$60.00	$455.00

Mileage Tracker

When keeping records of mileage for end of the year taxes, it's also important to be detailed. Write down the date, location of the event, your car's mileage before leaving, and again upon returning. Then make a note of the total miles driven. This is something you want to do after each event in order to make it a habit, but it will also be a lot easier to tally up than trying to figure out 12 months of mileage totals at one time at the end of the year.

Be honest with this, but also consider all of the driving involved in your business. Gas ain't cheap and a bit of a write off in this department can definitely help your bottom line. It will also offer you a good perspective on which shows and events are actually worth driving to if they are a long distance from home.

Travel to and from shows, events that you teach, or trips to the post office to mail out orders are all valid examples of what you can record. Keep in mind that if the post office is on your way to visit a friend or one of your stops before grocery shopping and other errands, you would only record your 1 way distance to the post office. For example: the post office is 4 miles from your house, so if you're off to mail this week's bundle of orders and going straight home after, you would record 8 miles total. However, if you are stopping at the store after, and then picking up your child from school, only record 4 miles.

This can simply be jotted down in a mini notebook that you keep in your car with a pen or pencil. (Friendly side note tip- I keep a mechanical pencil in the car because I live in the South and the summer heat destroys pens.)

Date:
Location:
Starting Mileage:
Ending Mileage:
Total Miles Driven:

Keeping Inventory Records

About 2 weeks ago I filed my yearly taxes and had a bit of a surprise. The tax specialist I had been working with for the last 6 years retired, and I have to admit that I was nervous about working with someone new. Everything went perfectly fine and I am relieved to say that I plan to use this new specialist for years to come. Why am I sharing this? Well, to say that sometimes change is good, but also this new person shared some tips with me that I think will definitely help my business this year, including that he mentioned keeping records of *cost of goods sold*. This can feel a bit confusing, but for our purposes here, it's basically keeping inventory.

I've already shared how you can keep track of your material and supply receipts, but as your business grows and those receipts continue to add up, you'll want to know how much of your supplies are new each year, and how much of your handmade goods are residual income from the previous year.

Think about it this way; if you purchased $1000 in supplies to make candles in December of 2021, but don't actually sell any of those candles until January or later in 2022, you'll be showing a large supply cost without an equal or greater amount of sales at the end of 2021, but then a larger amount of sales vs supplies in 2022 for these particular products. This is normal and with any business you would see this sort of ebb and flow. This is why retail stores do inventory counts at the end of each year or sometimes on a quarterly basis. Most of this is tracked in computer systems these days, but with handmade goods, it will probably be slightly less convenient to inventory supplies.

Why is it important? Because if year after year you show high supply and material costs without showing sales that make sense to the ebb and flow, it could be major red flags for an audit. I'm going to use jewelry making as an example of how to break down material costs and inventory, because it's something I am very familiar with and also I think it's probably one of the most tedious to deal with considering all of the little bits and pieces. So it should give you a solid concept for any business.

Initially when I purchase any findings (ear wires, jump rings, chain, beads, etc.) I separate each item into plastic compartmentalized jewelry bins and label exactly how much each little piece costs. So if a pack of 10 ear wires cost $4.00, I place a small sticker with $.40 each above them. This is super helpful when deciding how much to charge for a piece because I know exactly how much it cost me to make it. One step further, it now helps to tally up inventory at the end of the year.

I wouldn't suggest breaking down your inventory sheet into every bead and jump ring; who the heck has time for that! This year, I simply added up the total estimate for each bin. I also condensed all previously purchased items into a few bins, (labeling them as purchased before 2022) leaving plenty of room for new materials. This ensures that when I take inventory at the end of 2022, on whatever might be left, I am not re-claiming these previously purchased and claimed materials for a write off.

Once you have a handle on all of your supply bits, you'll also want to take stock of finished items that you haven't sold yet, but are ready to go in the new year. Go through all finished pieces and write down their retail values. The amount you will sell them for is what we're focusing on here, not the material cost.

Here is a sample chart of how I plan to keep records of my inventories from now on. I suggest finding an easy and clear way to organize whatever supplies you use for your work and then decide the easiest way to break down your inventory sheet.

Inventory on December 31st_____

Materials	Total Cost	Finished Items	Retail Value
Jewelry findings bin 1	$30	All earrings	$180
Jewelry findings bin 2	$25	All necklaces	$200
Jewelry findings bin 3	$10	All bracelets	$150
Beads bin 1	$40	Bookmarks	$200
Beads bin 2	$15		
Charms bin 1	$25		
Other/Misc	$25		

You would complete this every December 31st to end and begin the following year.

Final Thoughts

I hope that this book has helped you in some way to organize your business paperwork. Paperwork can sometimes be the creative person's worst nightmare, but I believe that with a system in place that works for you, it can make life much easier. If you're interested in a more detailed look into starting a handmade business focused around craft shows, or using craft shows to promote your online business, please take a look at my book, *A Guide to Craft Show Success,* by Sandra Belz, also available on Amazon. I wish you much success in your handmade business!

Where you can find me online:

Instagram: @BohoJouel

Shop BohoJouel Handmade and Fair Trade: https://bohojouel.shop

Shop with me on Etsy: https://www.etsy.com/shop/bohojouel

YouTube: BohoJouel

Made in the USA
Columbia, SC
11 March 2023